Workshop on the Role of Authoritative Standards in the MT Environment 2018

Held at AMTA 2018

Boston, Massachusetts, USA
17 March 2018

ISBN: 978-1-5108-6728-4

Workshop on the Role of Authoritative Standards in the MT Environment 2018

Held at AMTA 2018

Boston, Massachusetts, USA
17 March 2018

The 13th Conference of
The Association for Machine Translation
in the Americas
www.conference.amtaweb.org

WORKSHOP PROCEEDINGS
March 17, 2018

The Role of Authoritative Standards in the MT Environment

Organizer: Jennifer DeCamp *(MITRE)*

Authoritative Standards in the MT Environment

Workshop March 17, 2018

Jennifer DeCamp
Sue Ellen Wright
David Filip
Bill Rivers
Arle Lommel
Alan Melby

Overview

In this workshop, we bring together experts from across the standards community, including from the American Society for Testing and Materials (now just "ASTM International"), the American National Standards Institute (ANSI), the International Organization for Standardization (ISO), the Globalization and Localization Association (GALA), and the World Wide Web Consortium (W3C). These experts discuss authoritative standards that impact the development, implementation, and evaluation of translation systems and of the interoperability of resources.

The workshop consists of one-half day of technical presentations with invited talks on topics including the structure of the U.S. and international standards community, developing and implementing standards for translation quality assessment and quality assurance, the Translation API Class and Cases (TAPICC) initiative, and updates to Term Based eXchange (TBX). A panel discusses gaps in this network of standards. They also solicit input from co-panelists and from the audience on how to improve the standards and standards processes, particularly in the fast-changing world of semantic and neural technological development. Feedback will be provided to the relevant standards committees.

Participants

- Jennifer DeCamp   MITRE
- Alan K. Melby   LTAC Global
- Arle Lommel   Common Sense Advisory
- David Filip   Adapt Center
- Bill Rivers   Joint National Committee for Languages
- Sue Ellen Wright   Kent State University

Agenda, Presentations, and Page Numbers

Authoritative Standards in the MT Environment

Dr. Jennifer DeCamp

jdecamp@mitre.org

March 17, 2018

Association for Machine Translation in the Americas

Boston, MA

The author's affiliation with The MITRE Corporation is provided for identification purposes only, and is not intended to convey or imply MITRE''s concurrence with, or support for, the positions, opinions or viewpoints expressed by the author.
Approved for Public Release; Distribution Unlimited. Case Number 18-0342

How are Standards Important for MT?

1. Help with data and system interoperability

2. Implemented in software we want to use—so we deal with them whether or not we want to

3. Provide higher reliability/certainty than other methods of language ID, data exchange, and term retrieval

4. Provide guidance, replicability, and comparability in assessments

5. Sometimes cited/required in Requests for Proposal or in contracts—must show compliance

   - Direct specification
   - Minimal technical proficiency, minimal cost; technical delta; etc.

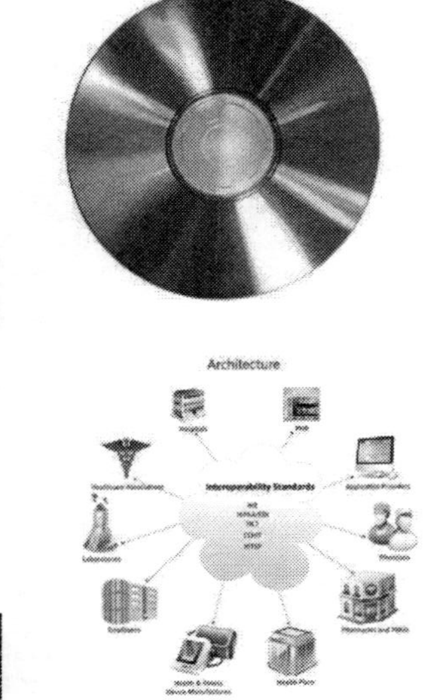

Fragmentation, Heterogeneity, and Non-Interoperability

"Current approaches to Machine Translation (MT) or professional translation evaluation, both automatic and manual, are characterized by

- A high degree of fragmentation, heterogeneity and a lack of interoperability between methods, tools and data sets.

- As a consequence, it is difficult to reproduce, interpret, and compare evaluation results."

Georg Rehm, Aljoscha Burchardt, Ondˇrej Bojar, Christian Dugast,Marcello Federico, Josef van Genabith, Barry Haddow, Jan Hajiˇc, Kim Harris, Philipp Koehn, Matteo Negri, Martin Popel, Lucia Specia, Marco Turchi, Hans Uszkoreit, **Translation Evaluation: From Fragmented Tools and Data Sets to an Integrated Ecosystem, Workshop held at LREC, 24 May 2016.**

Increasing Collaboration of MT and CAT

- MT increasingly used in commercial environments
- Agile configurations of MT and Computer Assisted Translation (CAT)
  - MT as an option in CAT
  - Predictive MT in CAT
  - Documents with different parts done with different methods
  - Decisions of customer or service provider of tools to use
- Need for evaluations that encompass many approaches or that are neutral to the approach

This Photo by Unknown Author is licensed under CC BY-NC-SA

7

Translation Quality

- ASTM F2575 *Standard Guide for Quality Assurance in Translation*
- ASTM WK 41374 *Standard Practice for Language Service Companies*
- ASTM WK 46396 *New Practice for the Development of Translation Q Metrics*
- ASTM Work Item (WK) 47362 *Standard Practice for Quality Assuranc Translation*
- ISO/AWI 21999 *Translation Quality Assurance and Assessment—Models and Metrics*
- ASTM WI 54884 *New Guide for Public Language Quality Assessment (LQA) Methodology*
- ISO 17100:2017 *Translation Services—Requirements for Translation Services*
- ISO 18587 *Translation Services—Post-Editing of Machine Translation Output— Requirements*
- TAUS *Multidimensional Quality Metrics* (MQM) and DFKI work
- TAUS, GALA, LT-Innovate *Translation API Class and Cases Initiative* (TAPICC)

Interoperability

- ISO 639-3, Codes for the Representation of Names of Languages
- IETF BCP 47 Tags for Identifying Languages
- Translation Memory eXchange (TMX)
- ISO 21720 XML Localization Interchange File Format (XLIFF)
- ISO 24613:2008 Lexical Markup Framework
- Translation API Class and Cases (TAPICC) Initiative

This Photo by Unknown Author is licensed under CC BY-SA

How it Works Together

So Why This Workshop?

- Provide you with examples of how standards can affect your work with MT

- Encourage debate on the best technical approaches for achieving
  - Interoperability with data and tools
  - Comparability and replicability with evaluations
  - Best practice

- Solicit your participation in development of key standards

Participants

- **Jennifer DeCamp**
  - Chair, ATA Standards Committee
  - Member ISO, ASTM, ANSI, ILR, AMTA, and ATA
  - Chair, ASTM TAG to ISO/TC 37/SC 4
  - Principal Scientist, MITRE Corporation

- **Sue Ellen Wright**
  - Chair, ASTM U.S. TAG to ISO/TC 37
  - Chair, ISO/TC 37/SC 3
  - Member ISO, ASTM, ANSI, and ATA
  - Professor, Translation Studies, Kent State University
  - Recipient of ANSI Outstanding Achievement Award

- **David Filip**
  - OASIS XLIFF OMOS TC Chair
  - OASIS XLIFF TC Secretary, Editor, Liaison Officer
  - Spokes Research Fellow
  - ADAPT Centre
  - KDEG, Trinity College Dublin

- **Bill Rivers**
  - Secretary, U.S. Technical Advisory Group to ISO/TC 37
  - Member ASTM, ANSI, ISO, and ATA
  - Executive Dir., Joint National Committee for Languages

- **Arle Lommel**
  - Project Leader for ASTM Translation Metrics Standard
  - Senior Analyst, Common Sense Advisory
  - Member ASTM, ATA, GALA

- **Alan Melby**
  - Liaison between ATA and FIT
  - Member ISO, ASTM, ANSI, OASIS, and ATA
  - President, LTAC
  - Associate Director, BYU Translation Research Group

Agenda

• **Jennifer DeCamp**	Introduction
• **Jennifer DeCamp**	Language Codes
• **Sue Ellen Wright**	TermBased eXchange (TBX)
• **Bill Rivers**	Translation Quality Standards
• **Arle Lommel**	Translation Metrics
• **Alan Melby**	Translation API for Class and Cases (TAPICC)
• **Panel**	

Questions for Possible Discussion

- What role will standards have to play in the future?
- Are there viable and preferable alternatives to using standards?
- How can we make the standards more useful to the translation environment, particularly with MT?
- Where do we have gaps or issues?
- Where do we need additional work?
- Do we have the right organizations represented?
- Do we have the right people working on the standards?

ISO Language Codes

Dr. Jennifer DeCamp

jdecamp@mitre.org

March 17, 2018

Association for Machine Translation in the Americas

Boston, MA

*The author's affiliation with The MITRE Corporation is provided for identification purposes only, and is not intended to convey or imply MITRE''s concurrence with, or support for, the positions, opinions or viewpoints expressed by the author.
Approved for Public Release; Distribution Unlimited. Case Number 18-0343'

Wherefore Language Codes?

- Demand by industry for codes for more languages
- Need for less ambiguity and overlap
- Need for linguistic rather than bibliographic orientation
  - Machine Readable Cataloging (MARC 21)
  - ISO 639-1 and ISO 639-2
  - Most commonly used system among linguists was The Ethnologue
- Need for consistency

Codes for the Representation of Language

- ISO 639-1   ar   Arabic
- ISO 639-2   ara   Arabic
- ISO 639-3   aeb   Tunisian Arabic
- ISO 639-5   ARA   Arabic, macrolanguage

- Four-letter codes for variants and registers?

- mis   Uncoded languages
- mul   Multilingual
- und   Undetermined languages
- xxx   No linguistic content/not applicable

ISO 639 Registrars and Joint Advisory Committee

PARTS

- ISO 639-1   Infoterm
- ISO 639-2   Library of Congress
- ISO 639-3   SIL International
- ISO 639-4   Joint
- ISO 639-5   Library of Congress
- ISO 639-6   TBD

- Joint Advisory Committee

International Engineering Task Force (IETF)
Best Current Practice (BCP) 47
Tags for Identifying Languages, 2009

- zh-Hans (Chinese written using the Simplified Chinese script)
- zh-cmn-Hans-CN (Chinese, Mandarin, Simplified script, as used in China)

- sr-Cyrl (Serbian written using the Cyrillic script)
- sr-Latn-RS (Serbian written using the Latin script as used in Serbia)

Request for Comment (RFC) 5646

- Language: fr (French)
- Language-Region: de-DE (German for Germany)
- Language subtag plus Script subtag: zh-Hant (Chinese written using the Traditional Chinese script)
- Extended language subtags and their primary language subtag counterparts: zh-cmn-Hans-CN (Chinese, Mandarin, Simplified script, as used in China)
- Language-Script-Region: zh-Hans-CN (Chinese written using the Simplified script as used in mainland China)
- Language-Variant: sl-rozaj (Resian dialect of Slovenian) sl-rozaj-biske (San Giorgio dialect of Resian dialect of Slovenian) sl-nedis (Nadiza dialect of Slovenian)
- Language-Variant: sl-rozaj (Resian dialect of Slovenian) sl-rozaj-biske (San Giorgio dialect of Resian dialect of Slovenian) sl-nedis (Nadiza dialect of Slovenian)

Status

- Correlated with many other standards
- Worldwide use
- Implemented for two decades in Microsoft, depending on keyboard
- ISO 639 up for review
  - Meetings in March to discuss processes
- New ISO standards in development to supplement ISO 639
  - Variants
  - Registers

Issues

- Not coordinated with speech community

- Variable width difficult to implement with older databases

- Too few Q codes

- People repurposing codes because they like the mnemonics or because they are trying to express dialects or other information within the three-character format

- Difficult to meet requirements for new codes (although easier than it used to be!)

Why is ISO 639 important for MT?

- Automatic language identification
  - Is not available for all languages and dialects
  - Is not always possible with very small numbers of words
- Correctly tagged text needed, particularly in languages with less textual material, for
  - Identification of text
  - Application of tools
- Incorrectly tagged text can result in
  - Use of wrong tools on the data (e.g., spellchecker)
  - Use of data incorrectly (e.g., in Translation Memories)

References

- IETF BCP 47 (2009). *Tags for Identifying Languages*, 2009.

- ISO15924, International Organization for Standardization, ISO 15924:2004. *Information and documentation -- Codes for the representation of names of scripts*, January 2004.

- ISO3166-1, International Organization for Standardization, ISO 3166-1:2006. *Codes for the representation of names of countries and their subdivisions -- Part 1: Country codes"*, November 2006.

- ISO639-1, International Organization for Standardization, ISO 639-1:2002. *Codes for the representation of names of languages -- Part 1: Alpha-2 code*, July 2002.

- ISO639-2, International Organization for Standardization, ISO 639-2:1998. *Codes for the representation of names of languages -- Part 2: Alpha-3 code*, October 1998.

- ISO639-3, International Organization for Standardization, ISO 639-3:2007. *Codes for the representation of names of languages - Part 3: Alpha-3 code for comprehensive coverage of languages*, February 2007.

- ISO639-4, International Organization for Standardization, ISO 639-4:2010. *Codes for the representation of names of languages - Part 3: Alpha-3 code for comprehensive coverage of languages*, February 2007.

- ISO639-5, International Organization for Standardization, ISO 639-3:2007. *Codes for the representation of names of macrolanguages- Part 5: Alpha-3 code for comprehensive coverage of languages*, February 2007.

Termbase eXchange (TBX)
Making Exchange Work for You

Dr. Sue Ellen Wright

Kent State University

March 18, 2018

Association for Machine Translation in the Americas

Boston, MA

Fragmentation, Heterogeneity, and Non-Interoperability

- Fragmentation, heterogeneity and a lack of interoperability between methods, tools and data sets (Jen's first slide)

- Applicable for termbase design as well

- Issues
  - TBX only viable for coherent data models
  - Prevalence of non-complying models
  - Lack of guidance regarding viable models
  - Need for coordination with XLIFF
  - Need for xmlns documentation
  - Outdated link handling

Increasing Collaboration of MT and CAT

- Agile combinations and recombinations of MT and Computer Assisted Translation (CAT)— difficult to separate out approaches except for limited evaluation of tools
  - MT as an option in CAT
  - Predictive MT in CAT
  - Role of terminology management in governing human interaction with MT and TM
  - Potential issue: interface between TBX & LMF

ISO 30042 – TermBase eXchange

- Issued in 2009, but subject to ongoing development
- New Draft International standard currently in ballot
- Archiving the information in a termbase
- Exchanging information between systems
  - Authoring (send monolingual information from a termbase to an authoring tool)
  - Translation (send a subset of the information from a termbase to a translator)
  - Data mining (export most/all information from a termbase for analysis using XML)
- Guiding the design of a new termbase for interoperability

ISO 30042 :2009– TermBase eXchange

- Positives
  - Powerful and flexible enough to express almost any termbase model
  - Viable for exchange among like data models & systems
- Negatives
  - Not widely used for exchange between divergent systems
  - Applications outputs not true TBX
  - TBX as a moving target
  - Exchange impossible between incompatible data models
  - Incompatibility with some modern xml solutions

TBX-Basic

- The localization industry solution to a normalized format
- "Dialect" of TBX consisting of a defined data model and a specified set of data categories
- Positive:
  - Standardized data model & selection of data categories (datcats)
  - Recognized user community
- Negative:
  - Rich, but restricted data category set
  - Need for reliable support tools
  - Some outdated XML conventions

TBX-Basic Dialect Boston, March 17 – 21, 2018
Concept Level
Subject field
Image
Note
Definition
Source of definition
Cross-reference/Reference
Creation Date
Created by
Last Modified Date
Last Modified by
Language Section
Language
Definition
Source
Note
Creation Date
Created by
Last Modified Date
Last Modified by
Term Section
Term
Source
Part of Speech
Gender
Usage Status
Term Type
Geographical Usage
Context
Source of context
Note
Cross-reference/Reference
Term Location
Customer
Project
External Cross-Reference

Support tools: tbxInfo.net

<TBX>   Home   About TBX ˅   Dialects ˅   Downloads ˅   Converters ˅   About Us ˅   Q

About TBX

˄ Purpose of TBX

˄ Importance of TBX

˅ Principles of TBX

TBX is an exchange format

TBX is an XML-based terminology exchange format, designed to make terminology databases easier and safer to maintain, distribute, and use.

TBX separates data from software

The TBX format is not dependent on any particular software application. TBX ensures that your termbase can be equally accessible via any software you prefer to use to access, display, update, or process your terminology.

Because TBX does not use a proprietary format, if you want to start using different termbase software, you can easily migrate your terminology. Any software with TBX support that you use will be able to access your termbase, leaving you free to change or update software while safeguarding your valuable termbases.

The TBX format is based in XML and encoded in Unicode, so it is even accessible by a text editor.

TBX protects data assets

Proprietary termbase file types can be lost if the associate software stops working because of technical or licensing issues. TBX doesn't have this risk—because TBX is a standardized, open-source file type, it can easily be read by any compatible tools or any number of open-source utilities.

TBXinfo.net screenshots with permission of LTAC Global

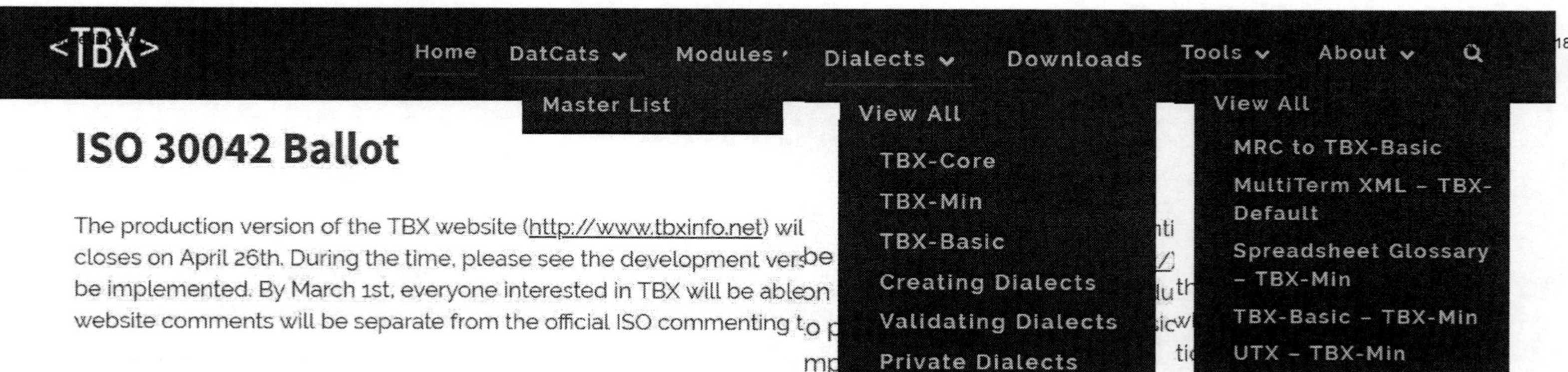

ISO 30042 Ballot

The production version of the TBX website (http://www.tbxinfo.net) wil closes on April 26th. During the time, please see the development ver be implemented. By March 1st, everyone interested in TBX will be able website comments will be separate from the official ISO commenting t

Any mention of **TBX Default** should be understood to refer to the master list of TBX data categories, rather than to a TBX dialect. Eventually (after the ballot ends in April), the website will be updated and the obsolete term TBX Default will no longer be mentioned except in historical notes.

TBX, or **TermBase eXchange**, is the international standard for *representing* and *exchanging* information about terminology.

The current version of the TBX standard was published in 2008. The next version is under development. In preparation for the next version, whenever you receive a TBX file, please check the value of the type attribute on the root element.

For example, in <martif type="TBX" xml:lang="en"> the type is simply TBX. The constraints on TBX are expected to be in an XCS file. However, in practice, the XCS file is often missing or not processed.

In the next version of TBX, the root element will be "tbx" instead of "mar dialect, for example "TBX-Basic". Each dialect name is associated with a modules. Each module clearly indicate which data categories are allow

http://www.tbxinfo.net

This change will address the single most common complaint about the current version of TBX: if there is no XCS file associated with a TBX document instance, you don't know what to expect. In the new version there is no XCS file; there is a dialect name; and you do know what to expect.

Upgrading and Empowering TBX

- ISO 30042:2018 and beyond

- Coordination with XLIFF terminology markup

- Use of xml namespaces

- Modernizing hypertext representations
  - TEI Term (ancestor of TBX) predated HTML & modern idref/href notations
  - /cross-reference/ envisioned as a datcat
  - Enabled by its own linking features

```
<descripSpec name="definition" datcatId="ISO12620A-0501">
    <contents/>
    <levels>langSet termEntry</levels>
</descripSpec>
<xrefSpec name="externalCrossReference" datcatId="ISO12620A-101807">
    <contents targetType="external"/>
</xrefSpec>
```

When TBX-Basic is not enough

- TBX-Linguist
  - Additional data categories
  - /figure/ added at the language level
  - /cross-reference/ swapped out for /related concept/ and /related term/
  - /register/
  - /grammaticalNumber/
  - /transferComment/
  - ja-specific datcats (reading, readingNote)

<TBX> TBX-Linguist

Filter/sorting fields

TBX-Basic	TBX-Linguist
Concept Level	
Subject Field	Subject Field
	Entry Identifier
Figure *	Figure*
Source of Figure*	Source
Note	Note
	Source
Definition	Definition
Source of Definition	Source
Related Concept	Related Concept
Customer Subset	Customer Subset
Project Subset	Project Subset
Created by	Created by
Last Modified Date	Last Modified Date
Last Modified by	Last Modified by*
External Cross-Reference	External Cross-Reference
Language Section	
Language	Language
Figure*	Figure*
Source of Figure*	Source
Definition	Definition
Source	Source
Note	Note
Source of Note*	Source
[Transaction Set]	[Transaction Set]

Language specific fields

TBX-Basic	TBX-Linguist
Term Section	
Term	Term
Source	Source
Part of Speech	Part of Speech
Gender	Gender
	Reading
	Reading Note
	Grammatical Number
Administrative Status	Term Status
Term Type	Term Type
Geographical Usage	Geographical Usage
	Usage Register
Context	Context
Source of Context	Source of context
Note	Note
Source of Note*	N-Source
Related Term	Related Term
	Transfer Comment
Term Location	Term Location
Customer Subset	Customer Subset
Project Subset	Project Subset
External Cross-Reference	External Cross-Reference
[Transaction Set]	[Transaction Set]

When TBX-Basic is not enough

- TBX-Linguist
  - Additional data categories
  - /figure/ added at the language level
  - /cross-reference/ swapped out for /related concept/ and /related term/
  - /register/
  - /grammaticalNumber/
  - /transferComment/
  - ja-specific datcats (reading, readingNote)

Figures at the Language Level

Entry number: 22

German

figure:

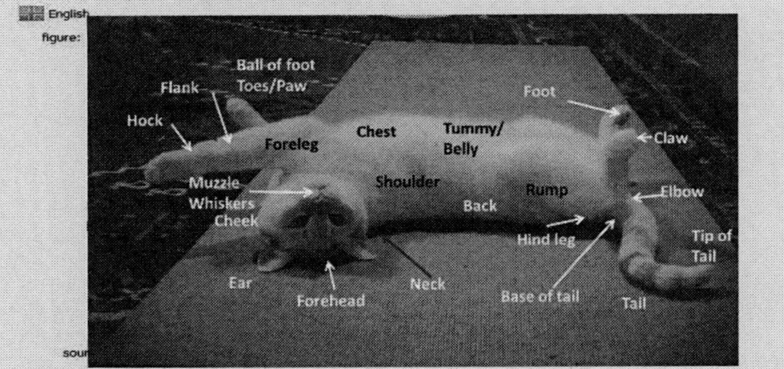

source: http://www.katzen-album.de/forum/viewtopic.php?t=24127 2017-07-13

definition: eine Familie (Félidae) der Raubtiere

source: http://www.wortbedeutung.info/Katze/ 2017-07-13

Term: Katze

partOfSpeech: noun

administrativeStatus: preferred

grammaticalGender: feminine

context: Mit ihren scharfen Krallen können Katzen sehr gut Bäume hochklettern, aber zum Abstieg muss die Katze gelernt haben, ihre nach vorne gekrümmten Krallen als „Steighaken" zu benutzen. Unerfahrene Katzen versuchen, mit dem Kopf voraus nach unten zu klettern, wobei sie schnell in Schwierigkeiten kommen können, in Panik geraten und in eine Schockstarre verfallen.

source: https://de.wikipedia.org/wiki/Katzen 2017-07-13

English

figure:

sour

definition: any of a family (Felidae) of carnivorous usually solitary and nocturnal mammals (such as the domestic cat, lion, tiger, leopard, jaguar, cougar, wildcat, lynx, and cheetah)

Term Entry Links

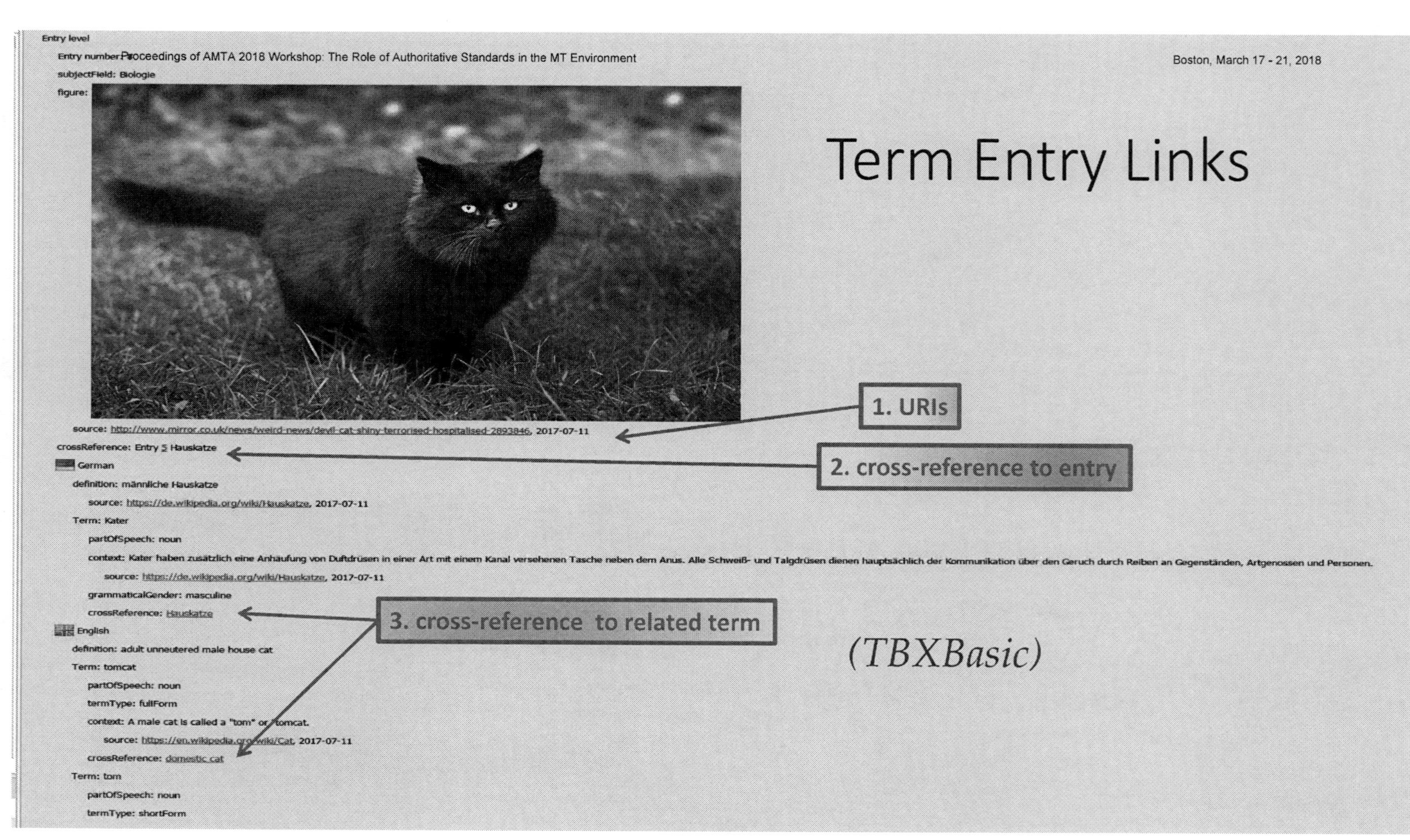

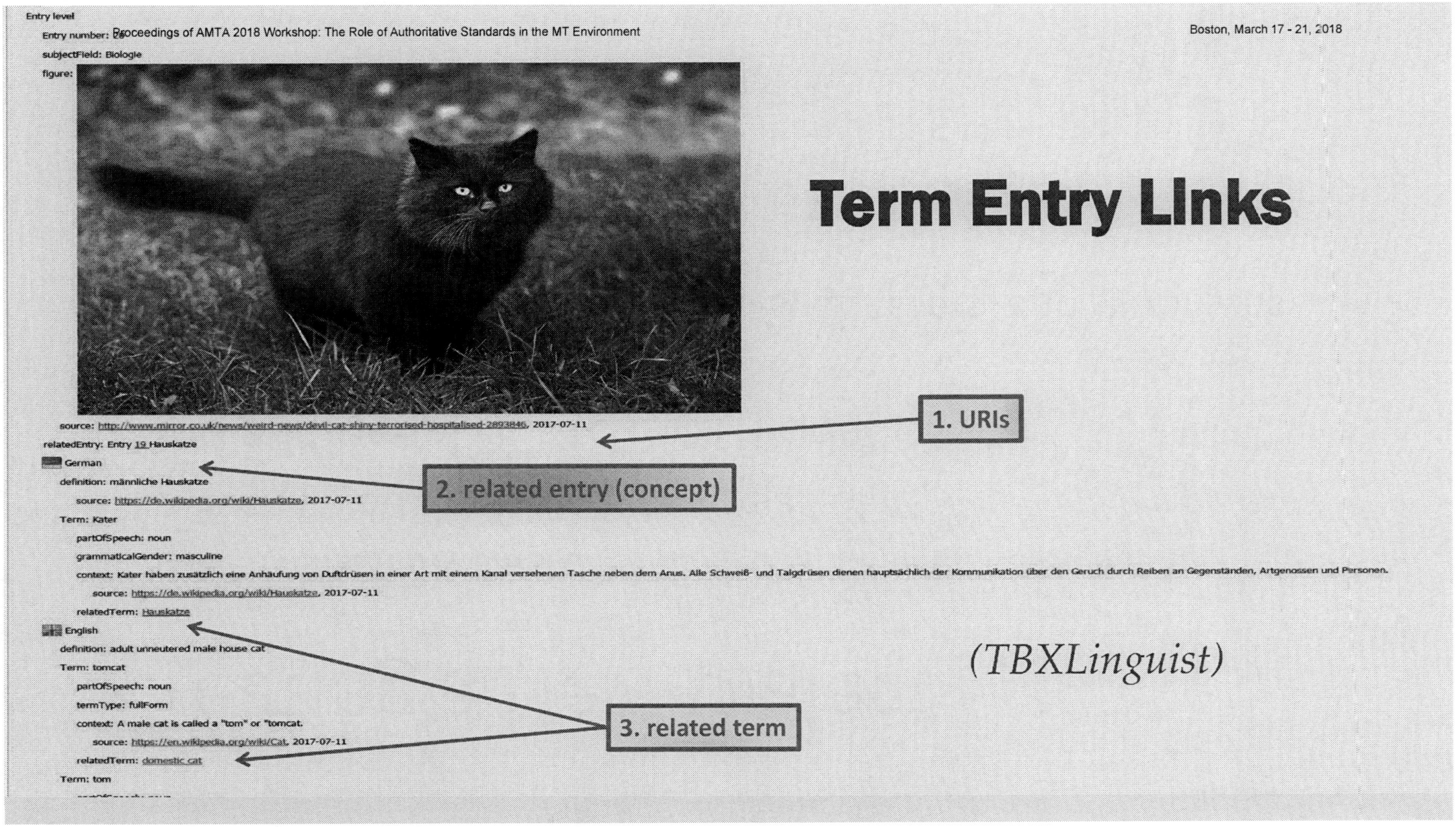
Term Entry Links
(TBXLinguist)
1. URIs
2. related entry (concept)
3. related term
Entry level
Entry number:
subjectField: Biologie
figure:
source: http://www.mirror.co.uk/news/weird-news/devil-cat-shiny-terrorised-hospitalised-2893846, 2017-07-11
relatedEntry: Entry 19 Hauskatze
German
definition: männliche Hauskatze
source: https://de.wikipedia.org/wiki/Hauskatze, 2017-07-11
Term: Kater
partOfSpeech: noun
grammaticalGender: masculine
context: Kater haben zusätzlich eine Anhäufung von Duftdrüsen in einer Art mit einem Kanal versehenen Tasche neben dem Anus. Alle Schweiß- und Talgdrüsen dienen hauptsächlich der Kommunikation über den Geruch durch Reiben an Gegenständen, Artgenossen und Personen.
source: https://de.wikipedia.org/wiki/Hauskatze, 2017-07-11
relatedTerm: Hauskatze
English
definition: adult unneutered male house cat
Term: tomcat
partOfSpeech: noun
termType: fullForm
context: A male cat is called a "tom" or "tomcat.
source: https://en.wikipedia.org/wiki/Cat, 2017-07-11
relatedTerm: domestic cat
Term: tom

Creating a New Dialect

- Start from TBX Basic
  - Even if you don't want to use all of it!
- Add additional DCs to data model
- Map any name changes
- Edit data model for all languages, all terms, and synonyms for each language
- Activate datcats in the respective model levels

Creating a New Dialect

- Update
  - Data model (previous slide)
  - Layout model (replicate additions at all levels)
  - Input model
    - You can leave out items you don't want to use in a given iteration
    - But keep them in the core data model & in layout
- Edit TBX-Basic output xml as needed (datcat names)
- Import seamlessly into new data model

Honor the telescope!

- TBX Core + TBX^{Min} + TBX^{Basic} + TBX^{Linguist} Modules = TBX-Linguist Dialect
- Each successive dialect is a superset of what comes before
- All subordinate dialects can be imported into the final component
- Additional data categories in the final component are identified and can if desired be manipulated by conversion routines.

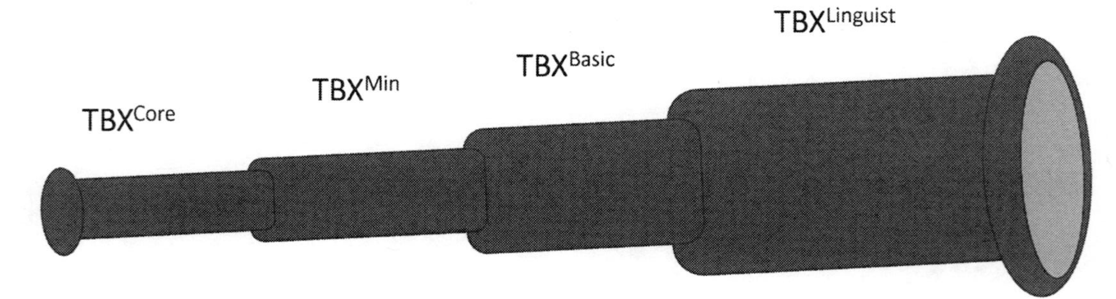

Structural Integrity

- TBX-Basic fully included sub-set of TBX-Linguist
- Some names changed—mapped to existing names
- Cross-reference involves a structural change
- Some items could be omitted from an input model or display (e.g., /term location/, (term) source)
- Slides 9 & 10 illustrate smooth import

Tools Issues

- Modify support tools to accommodate new data profile as a superset of TBXBasic
- Lean to rich (if properly mapped) facilitates clean exchange
- Rich to lean – possible tool to convert missing datcats to notes
- Possible if the tool knows about the other dialect

Additional Issues

- Concept relations (I-Term, Coreon) and knowledge modeling datcats are currently excluded from the TBX master file.
- Bibliography entries incorporated in termbases are not part of the encoding scheme.
- Coordination with MT component of hybrid CAT/MT?
- Coordination with LMF?

Contact Information

- Sue Ellen Wright
  swright@kent.edu

Miss Gina makes her appearance here thanks to the kind permission of her mistress, Jennifer Winer.

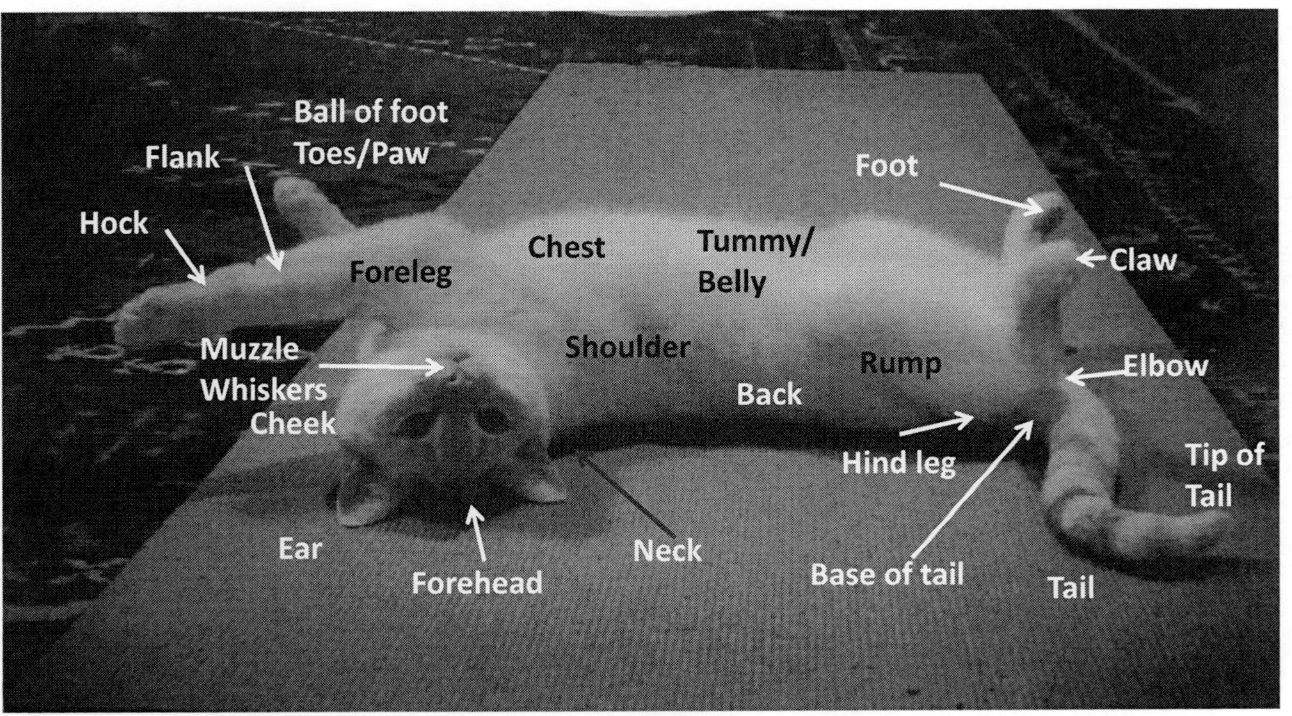
Ball of foot
Toes/Paw
Flank
Foot
Hock
Chest
Tummy/
Belly
Foreleg
Claw
Muzzle
Shoulder
Rump
Elbow
Whiskers
Cheek
Back
Hind leg
Tip of
Tail
Ear
Neck
Base of tail
Tail
Forehead

XLIFF 2 slides for AMTA Standards Workshop

Dr. David Filip

ADAPT Centre

OASIS XLIFF TC, OASIS XLIFF OMOS TC, GALA TAPICC SC, NSAI expert to
ISO TC 37 & ISO/IEC JTC 1 /WG 9, /SC 38, /SC 42

What's XLIFF?

[Do we need this slide? Demographics of the room..]

- XML Localiz(s)ation Interchange File Format
- The only ***open standard* *bitext format***
- XLIFF lives in OASIS since 2001
- First fully standardized as XLIFF 1.2 in February 2008
- XLIFF 2.0 August 2014
- XLIFF 2.1 February 2018

XLIFF 2

XLIFF Version 2.1
OASIS Standard
13 February 2018

http://docs.oasis-open.org/xliff/xliff-core/v2.1/os/xliff-core-v2.1-os.html
http://docs.oasis-open.org/xliff/xliff-core/v2.1/os/xliff-core-v2.1-os.pdf
http://docs.oasis-open.org/xliff/xliff-core/v2.1/os/xliff-core-v2.1-os.xml
XML schemas: http://docs.oasis-open.org/xliff/xliff-core/v2.1/os/schemas/

http://docs.oasis-open.org/xliff/xliff-core/v2.1/os/xliff-core-v2.1-os.html#mediaType

What's new compared to 1.2

Overall: Focus on the "naïve" implementer, don't assume tribal knowledge

- **Fixed inline data model [NOT** BACKWARDS COMPATIBLE**]**

- **Explicit** fragment identification mechanism
  -> **IANA registration of media type [*.xlf]**
  provisional for 2.0 -> permanent for 2.1

- Re-segmentation [**segmentation modification**] capability
  [NOT BACKWARDS COMPATIBLE**]**

- Better managed extensibility **[NOT** BACKWARDS COMPATIBLE**]**

- Advanced Constraints and Processing Requirements
  -> **Enforceable Conformance Clause**

What's new compared to 2.0

Overall: All XLIFF 2 is and will be backward & forwards compatible

- IANA registration of media type [*.xlf]
provisional for 2.0 -> **permanent as of XLIFF Version 2.1 for 2.0 and higher**

- Better managed extensibility [since 2.0]
-> Demoted 2.0 Change Tracking Module to an extension
-> Promoted **ITS 2.0** extension to a **huge and powerful module in 2.1**

- Advanced Constraints and Processing Requirements
-> Enforceable Conformance Clause [since 2.0]
-> Translated the human readable conformance requirements into **an exhaustive set of fully machine readable declarative validation artifacts**
-> enables complex automated roundtrip workflows relying on strict validity

Why should MT implementers care for XLIFF?

- XLIFF has a **simple and efficient inline data model** capable of **representing any content formats**, well formed or not
  - Native code representation – masking
  - **Powerful annotation mechanism with standoff capability**
    Localization Note | Terminology | Text Analytics
    Subsegment or supersegment Matching | Custom annotations | State and substate
    MT Confidence | Localization Quality Issue [MQM] & Rating | Provenance

- XLIFF is **bitext**, therefore **alignment** of source and target segments is **100% guaranteed**

- XLIFF is extremely **metadata rich**, hence suitable for on the fly **creation of custom corpora**
  Domain | Terminology | Language tags | Quality | Provenance

XLIFF 2 data model reuse

- Industry and public sector fast to adopt the superior XLIFF 2 data model. Desire to unleash the XLIFF 2 data model goodne, free it from XMLisms and SGMLisms ;-)

  -> Formation of OASIS XLIFF OMOS TC

  - https://www.oasis-open.org/apps/org/workgroup/xliff-omos/
  - https://github.com/oasis-tcs/xliff-omos-om
  - https://github.com/oasis-tcs/xliff-omos-jliff

- **JLIFF feeds into TAPICC Tracks 2 & 3**

  - Real time exchange of data at unit level
  - While XLIFF mandates the whole document structure, JLIFF is specifically defined as a ***Fragment*** Interchange format [JSON Localization Interchange Fragment Format]

Q&A

Quality Standards for Translation in ASTM & ISO

Dr. Bill Rivers

Executive Director, Joint National Committee for Languages

Former Chair, ASTM F43 on Language Services and Products

March 17, 2018

Overview

- Intro to JNCL-NCLIS
- Industry consensus standards
- ASTM & ISO standards for translation
- Common principles

An introduction first...

- **JNCL-NCLIS**
  - Founded 1974 by ACTFL, AATF, AATG, AATI, AATSEEL, AATSP, ATJ, MLA, NCLG, NMFLTA, TESOL
  - Works to develop policy recommendations (JNCL) and advocate for them to the US Government and business community (NCLIS)
- 140+ member organizations
- Exec. Dir., Dr. Rivers, served as founding chair of ASTM F43, 2011-2017

Industry Consensus Standards

- Voluntary
- Negotiated to consensus among stakeholders
    - Providers
    - Purchasers
    - Regulators & researchers
- Consensus ≠ unanimity, BUT
    - Due process is guaranteed
- Started with steel (1898); quality management and services added in the past ~35 years

What is ASTM? ISO?

- ASTM: formerly the American Society for Testing and Materials
  - Founded in 1898
  - outgrowth of early efforts at industry consensus standards
  - Oldest international standards development body
  - Based in US but international in scope
  - Membership open to all; individual and organizational members
- International Standards Organisation:
  - Established 1947
  - International NGO
  - Membership is at the national level (ANSI, BSI, Standards Canada)

Types of Standards for T & I

- ASTM
  - Standard Practice: Can be
    - Referenced in a contract, audited by one or another party
    - Organization can be certified to a Standard Practice by a third party, irrespective of a specific contract/project
  - Standard Guide:
    - Serves as information on "best practices"
    - Organizations may indicate that the **adhere to** a Standard Guide
    - Cannot be certified
- ISO:
  - International Standard: All ISs are certifiable at the organizational level, by third party certifying bodies

Current Standards

- ASTM
  - Under the jurisdiction of ASTM F43 on Language Services and Products
  - ASTM F2575-14, Standard Guide for Quality Assurance in Translation
  - ASTM WK54884, Standard Practice for Linguistic Quality Assessment Framework
- ISO: Under the jurisdiction of ISO TC 37, Committee on Language and Terminology, SC 5 on Translation and Interpreting
  - International Standard: ISO 17100:2015, Translation Services: Requirements for Translation Services
  - International Standard: ISO 18587:2017, Translation Services — Post-editing of Machine Translation Output — Requirements

ASTM F2575 Standard Practice for Language Translation

Content:

> Terminology
> Significance and Use
> Specifications
> Phases of a Translation Project

ASTM F2575 Standard Practice for Language Translation

Important issues:

- Definition of translation
- Indicators of translator competence
- Other participants in process
- Translation technology
- Services related to translation
- Post-project review

ASTM WK54884, Standard Practice for Linguistic Quality Assessment

- Establishes a practice for graduated, holistic rating of quality of translation
- Four categories:
  - Readability (P/F)
  - Accuracy
  - Linguistic conformity
  - Absence of fatal errors
- Error typology-agnostic
- Crowd-sourced, subjective, and statistically analyzed
  - Expert or non-expert
- Major clients using this now (Fortune 100; ACA en español)

Common principles

- ASTM F2575 & ISO standards seek to _assure_ quality through standardization of the delivery of the service
  - Personnel qualifications
  - Project specifications
  - Agreed-upon delivery and satisfaction criteria
  - Anomaly reporting & correction
- ASTM WK54884 seeks to standardize the _assessment_ of translation output

Ok, but some of the Standard won't work for our situation

- In general: exceptions to the standard must be documented and justified:
  - E.g., personnel qualifications in low-density languages
- Systematic/organizational vs. specific/situational exceptions
- Longer term: work on improving the standard
  - Join ASTM F43 (open to all)
  - Let the US Technical Advisory Group to ISO TC37 know what needs work

Contact:

Bill Rivers

wrivers@languagepolicy.org

Translation Quality Standards

Dr. Arle Lommel

alommel@csa-research.com

March 17, 2018

Association for Machine Translation in the Americas

Boston, MA

This presentation covers*

Feature	WD ISO 21999	ISO 17100:2015	ASTM F2575-14	ASTM WK46396 (MQM-DQF)
Type and Status	Proposed committee draft for international standard (ballot closed)	International standard	Global standard (based on individuals and companies, rather than national bodies) — under revision.	Working draft based on industry standard from DFKI and TAUS
Guidance vs. requirements	Guidance	Requirements	Guidance, update will be requirements	Requirements (proposed)
Orientation (process vs. product)	Combination of process and product	Process (quality assurance)	Combination (primarily process)	Product
Includes quality metric?	Yes	No	No	Yes

- This presentation does not cover the following:
  ASTM WK41374, for language service companies standard, which adopts a business process approach (in final editing)
- ASTM WK54884, translation quality evaluation workflow (working draft)

Why do these standards matter for MT?

- Disconnect between MT development and commercial translation production that includes MT
  - Reference-based methods (such as BLEU et al.) is central to MT development
  - Reference-free quality evaluation is central to commercial translation production
  - See <u>MT Escaped from the Lab. Now What?</u> (Mike Dillinger, AMTA 2016)
- These standards are influential among *implementers* of MT
- Systematically improving MT requires knowledge about what MT does wrong and *why* one translation is better than another (requires analytic understanding)

What do we mean by translation quality?

Well, what do we mean by "translation"?

- A translation (product) is target-language content corresponds to source-language content
  - Must include text
  - May include non-textual elements such as audio-visual content and software components
- Translation (process) is the action of creating target-language content that corresponds to source-language content according a set of specifications

What is translation quality?

- A subject of debate and contention
- Multiple measurement approaches are current
- Major disconnect between traditional human translation approaches and what MT developers do
- No one-size-fits-all set of specifications (more later)

Process vs. product

Process-centric	Product-centric
Emphasize the role of process steps on output quality	Focus on measuring conformance of translated content
Repeatability and consistency are the key	Can measure how well processes are delivering on expectations
Cannot determine whether the output meets requirements	Cannot verify process compliance or suitability

Universal or specifications-based

Universal	Specifications
There exists a set of one or more translations that are correct in all circumstances	Translations must conform to specifications: What works for one set may not work for another
Translations are good or bad	Translations are good or bad with respect to external factors
You could apply one set of criteria to any translation	Different requirements need different criteria

Reference-based or reference-free

Reference-based	Reference-free
Quality is measured by similarity to a known-good translation	Quality is measured by examining the product itself
Quick and cheap	Comparatively expensive and slow
Gives a score for the translation as a whole with no insight into specific issues	Provides insight into specific issues and allows decomposition (roll-down) of scores
Common in the MT world	Common in the HT world

WD ISO 21999: Translation quality assurance and assessment — Models and metrics

A general framework for translation quality

- Defines quality-related terms
- Sets up criteria for:
  - Job assignment and acceptance
  - Style
  - Consistency
  - Terminology
- Establishes a process for quality assessment of translation
- Discusses methods

Status

- Currently a committee draft
- Working through the ISO process
- Proposes a high-level typology of errors that is broadly compatible with MQM-DQF

ISO 17100:2015: Translation services – Requirements for translation services

A process-oriented approach to quality

- Defines processes that translation providers should follow to produce appropriate output
- Certifiable standard
- Replaces EN15038
- Widely implemented by language service providers
- Not generally applicable to MT

ASTM F2575-14: Standard Guide for Quality Assurance in Translation

Defines a stakeholder-oriented approach

- Emphasizes the role of specifications and factors that stakeholders need to consider
- Defines 21 parameters that need to be defined for projects
  - These serve as the basis for the MQM-DQF approach
  - Cover linguistic, production, environment, and relationship factors
- Apply to all translation projects, but does not define metrics for measuring quality
- The approaches in F2575 are largely ignored in MT circles, which results in a lack of clarity

ASTM WK46396: MQM-DQF (Translation Quality Assessment)

The F43 approach to quality

- ASTM F43 takes a *functionalist* approach, consistent with quality management principles:

A quality translation demonstrates *accuracy* and *fluency* required for the *audience and purpose* and *complies with all other specifications* negotiated between the requester and provider, taking into account both *requester goals* and *end-user needs*.

Genesis of WK46396

- TAUS Dynamic Quality Framework (DQF)
  - Arose from industry group
  - Focused on multiple approaches to quality (adequacy and fluency, error review, productivity measurement, MT ranking, and comparison)
  - Contained a relatively simple error typology
- DFKI Multidimensional Quality Metrics (MQM)
  - funded by European Commission in the QTLaunchPad and QTLeap projects
  - Focused on an exhaustive and robust *typology* of translation errors divided into multiple dimensions
- Unified error typology in 2014–2015 as a requirement of the European Commission

Drafting committee

- **Alan Melby** (BYU and LTAC Global)
- **Arle Lommel** (CSA Research)
- **Kirill Soloviev** (ContentQuo)
- **Aljoscha Burchardt** (DFKI)
- **Hans Uszkoreit** (DFKI)
- **Ingemar Strandvik** (European Commission)

- **Jennifer DeCamp** (MITER Corp)
- **Susanne Hempel** (SAP)
- **David Koot** (TAUS)
- **Jaap van der Meer** (TAUS)
- **Merle Tenney** (independent)

Approaches to quality evaluation

- Emphasizes analytic quality (identification and quantification of errors)
- Applies to both machine and human translation: Complements reference-based approaches such as BLEU
- Strives for consistency with ISO 9000-series approaches to quality management
- Emphasizes fairness
- Optionally considers source text as well as target text

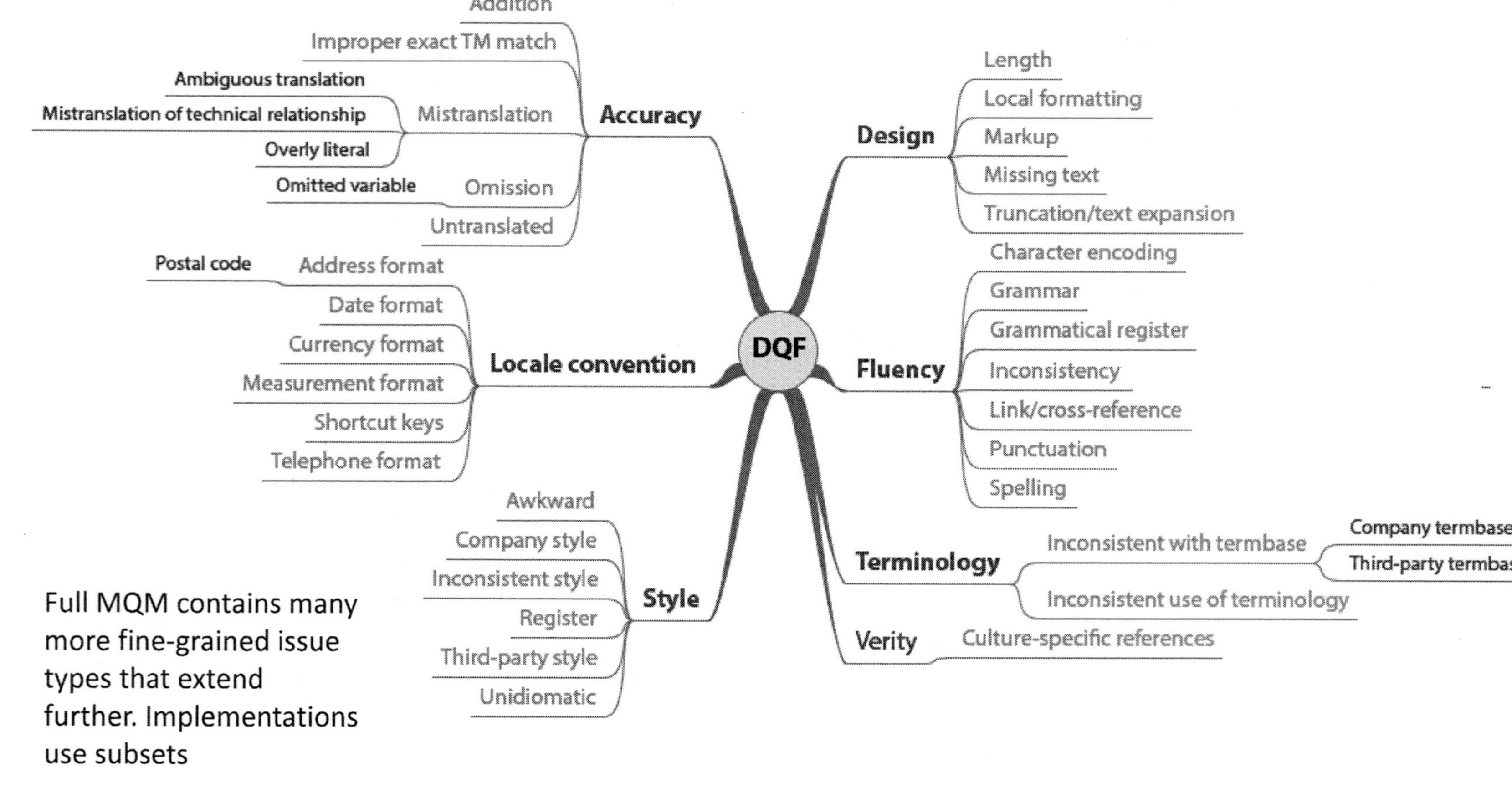

Full MQM contains many more fine-grained issue types that extend further. Implementations use subsets

Focus of ASTM effort

- How to create custom metrics based on MQM-DQF
- Tied to translation specifications as defined in ASTM F2575
- Currently working on a complete draft to be ready by October
- Error typology will be maintained in W3C Community Group to ensure free and open access
  - Required by IP donors and European Commission (MQM was taxpayer funded)
  - W3C connection will promote closer ties with other standardization efforts and increase visibility for the error typology

Adoption of MQM-DQF

- **LSPs and Enterprises**
  - Dell-EMC
  - eBay
  - LDS Church
  - Lionbridge
  - Microsoft
  - Moravia
  - Mozilla
  - Seprotec
  - Synergium
  - Tableau
  - Welocalize

- **Tools**
  - ContentQuo
  - MemSource
  - SDL (plug-in)
  - XTM

- **European projects**
  - QTLaunchpad
  - QT21

- Academia
  - Various projects

- **In process**
  - Argos Translations
  - Booking.com
  - CA Technologies
  - Capita
  - Crestec
  - DaimlerIntuit
  - John Deere
  - Nike
  - TNT-Fedex

Conclusion

Observations

- Translation quality is a hot topic
- A lot of people are trying to solve it
- The market is shifting towards MQM-DQF:
  - A good sign for the ASTM WK46349 effort
- ISO 17100 has high recognition among LSPs
- ISO 21999 is still in its infancy
- We still need to do more to bridge the gap between the BLEU/METEOR-centric approach of MT developers and the needs of consumers, translators, and LSPs

TAPICC initiative from GALA: AMTA 2018

Who in the MT community should care about TAPICC?

- Mike Dillinger (2016 AMTA keynote):
  - MT researchers and MT users very different goals

- MT researchers: "Build autonomous translation machines"
- MT users: "Integrate MT with workflow and human expertise"

- To MT researchers who have no desire to integrate their systems into a translation workflow: *Please take a nap during this presentation!*

Agenda

Who we are:
GALA and the TAPICC initiative

Why we're here:
Purpose of TAPICC + what's been done

The Ask:
Your feedback and involvement

What is GALA?

- Global non-profit trade association with membership of 400 companies (LSPs, tech developers, buyers of translation)

- Non-biased platform for information-sharing and collaboration, training, and professional development

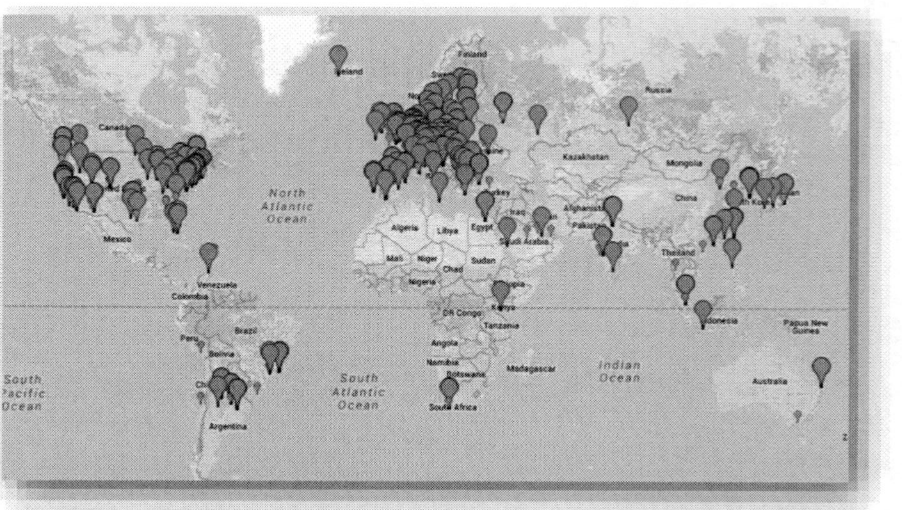

Partnerships and Complementary Initiatives

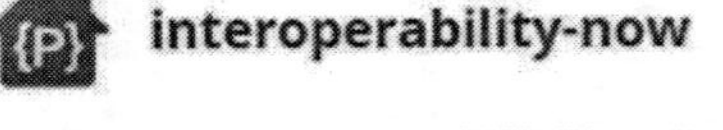

Boarding:
Why TAPICC?

- Are you a:
  - Supplier of MT output to end users?
  - System integrator tying a content management system (CMS) to a translation management system (TMS)?

How would you describe your experience?

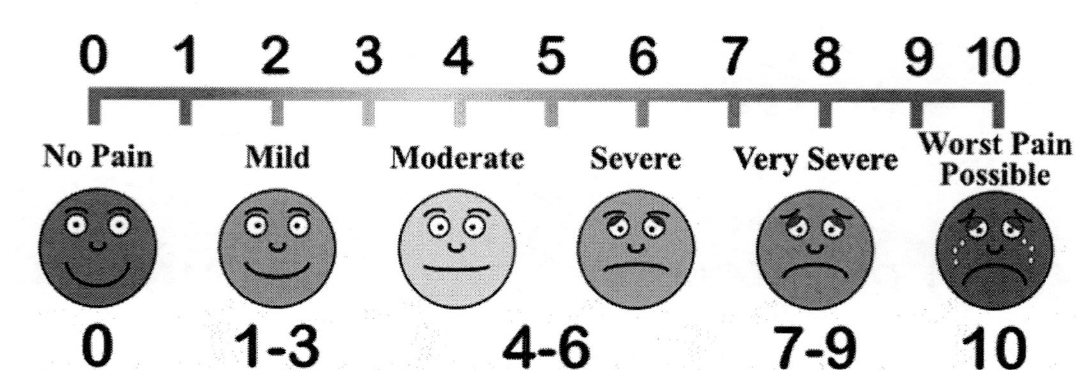

content management
tech and practices

the CMS/TMS gap

translation management
tech and practices

Starts with: "How do I translate the content that I'm managing in my CMS?"

- system-to-system communication
- automation

The Current API Wild West

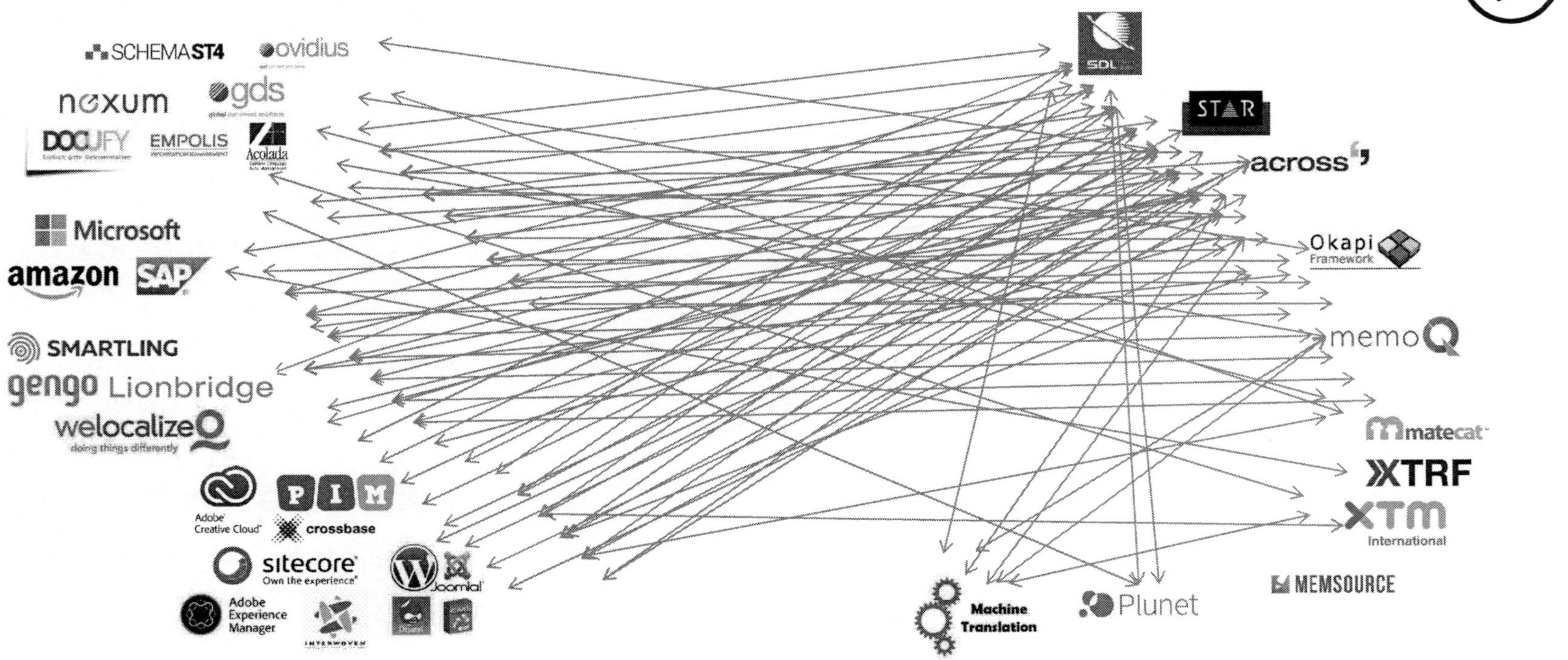

The Current API Wild West

- Unnecessary variation
- Continuous reinvention of the wheel
- Wasted $$!
  - For clients
  - For LSPs
  - For tools vendors
- Loss of operational freedom

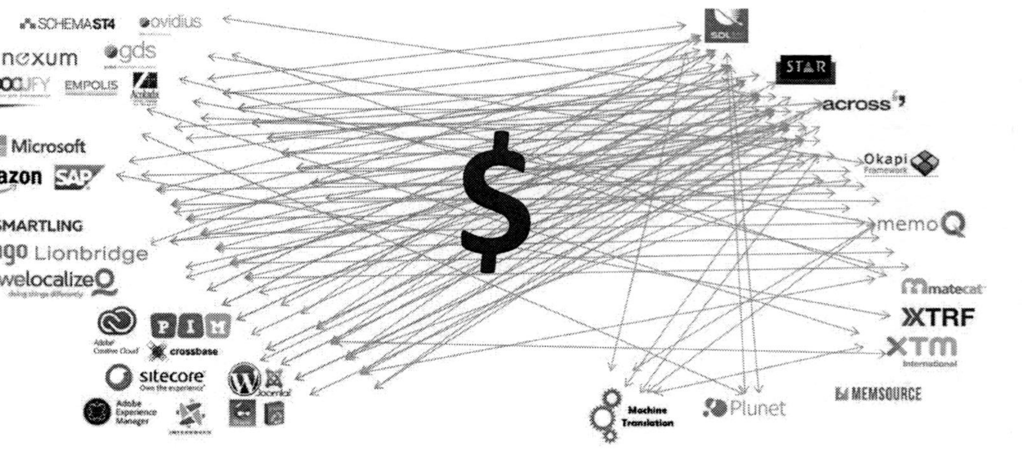

Can be a "deal breaker" for making content available worldwide!

www.gala-global.org/tapicc

The TAPICC Vision

Features & Benefits

Take-Off

First actions

Foundation

Legal Framework (Open Source)

- The 3-Clause BSD License (BSD-3 Clause)
- Creative Commons Legal Code (CC-BY 2.0)

Community Engagement

- GALA forum
- Working groups
- GitHub wiki
- Wide representation from the language industry

Organizational Documents

- Project charter
- Working Group Playbook
- Numerous presentations and marketing collateral

Four Tracks

1 Business metadata for supply chain automation
- Harmonize existing business metadata models

2 Exchange on unit level
- Pass a segment/unit from an editor to a TM/MT or other tool

3 Semantic enrichment of units
- Terminology, TM, MT, layout for "good enough"

4 Layout representation level
- Support process with visual context

www.gala-global.org/tapicc

Track 1: Four Working Groups

1. Business Metadata	2. Payload Specification	3. XLIFF Extraction	4. API Specification
• Define wrapper-level metadata • Canonical names and values • Workflow relevance • Harmonization • Compatibility	• Define types of payload • Define payload-level metadata • Canonical names and values • Harmonization • Compatibility	• Extraction guidance • ITS decoration • XLIFF Extractors/Mergers • XLIFF OM representations, e.g. JLIFF	• Protocols • Transfer, pull and/or push • Define classes • Code samples/ • snippets • Specify API

Each WG has co-chairs and 20+ participants. Join WG groups on GALA's website: www.gala-global.org/tapicc

TAPICC Deliverables so far...

- Business Glossary of Translation Industry by WG1
- Elementary Task types by WG1
- List of recommended payload types by WG2
- List of XLIFF extraction and merging Best Practices by WG3
- Data model and RESTful API data model draft by WG4

www.gala-global.org/tapicc

We need the interest and involvement of all stakeholders:

- Content publishers
- Integrators of MT systems
- Providers of localization and translation services ("LSPs")
- Localization tools architects and developers
- Multilingual content, software and process architects

The Asks

- Take interest in the initiative

- Follow the working groups
  ...or refer a colleague

- Review current drafts and provide feedback

TAPICC Resources

https://www.gala-global.org/TAPICC

- Project Charter
- Open Source Legal agreement
- Project Statement

- TAPICC Groups
- Various links

Thanks for your involvement!

Association for Computational Linguistics
209 N. Eighth Street
Stroudsburg, Pennsylvania 18360

ISBN 978-1-5108-6728-4